W9-BPQ-736

A Picture Book of
Helen Keller

David A. Adler

illustrated by John & Alexandra Wallner

Holiday House / New York

Other books in David A. Adler's *Picture Book Biography* series

A Picture Book of George Washington
A Picture Book of Abraham Lincoln
A Picture Book of Martin Luther King, Jr.
A Picture Book of Thomas Jefferson
A Picture Book of Benjamin Franklin

Text copyright © 1990 by David A. Adler
Illustrations copyright © 1990 by John C. and Alexandra Wallner
All rights reserved
Printed and Bound in August 2017 at Tien Wah Press, Johor Bahru, Johor, Malaysia.

17 18 19 20

Library of Congress Cataloging-in-Publication Data

Adler, David A.
A picture book of Helen Keller / written by David A. Adler;
illustrated by John and Alexandra Wallner.
p.   cm.
Summary: A brief biography of the woman who overcame her handicaps
of being both blind and deaf.
ISBN 0-8234-0818-3
1. Keller, Helen, 1880–1968.—Juvenile literature.   2. Blind-deaf—
United States—Biography—Juvenile literature.   [1. Keller, Helen,
1880–1968.   2. Blind.   3. Deaf.   4. Physically handicapped.]
I. Wallner, John C., ill.   II. Wallner, Alexandra, ill.   III. Title.
HV1624.K4A45   1990
362.4'1'092—dc20
[B]
[92]   89-77510   CIP   AC
ISBN-13: 978-0-8234-0818-4 (hardcover)
ISBN-13: 978-0-8234-0950-1 (paperback)   ISBN 0-8234-0950-3 (pbk.)

HOLIDAY HOUSE is registered in the U.S. Patent and Trademark Office.

Helen Keller was born in Tuscumbia, Alabama on June 27, 1880. She was a pretty baby. She was happy and smart.

When Helen was just six months old, she began talking. But a year later, in February 1882, she became sick. She had a high fever. Her parents and doctors were afraid she would die.

Helen's mother held her and placed wet towels on Helen's forehead to cool the fever. After a few days the illness was gone.

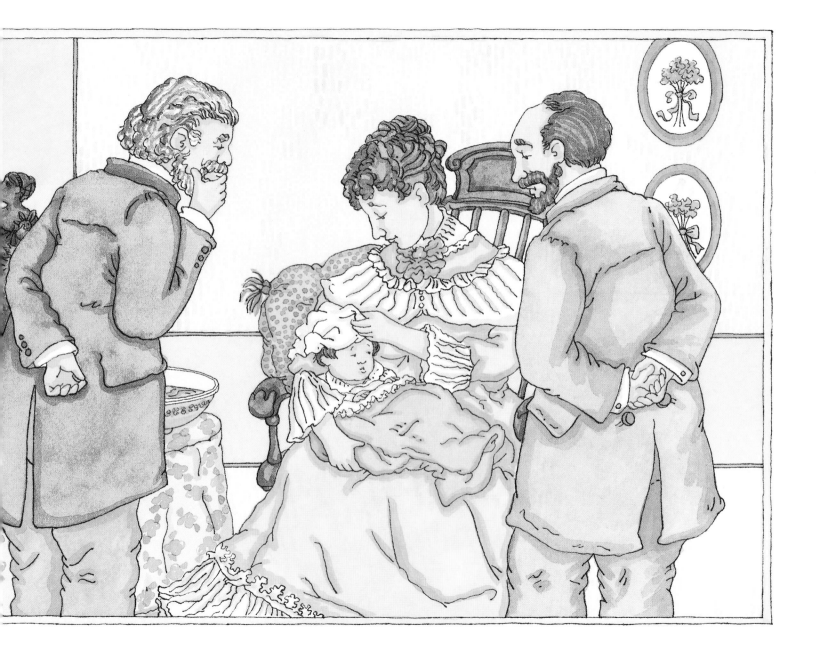

But Helen had changed. She turned away from bright lights. She didn't hear people when they spoke to her. The illness had left Helen Keller blind and deaf. The world for her became forever dark and quiet.

Because Helen could not hear other people speak, she did not learn to talk herself. She forgot the few words she knew as a baby. Helen did things with her hands to tell people what she wanted. Helen pretended to tie her hair in a bun if she wanted her mother. She pretended to cut and butter a slice of bread if she wanted bread.

Helen held onto her mother's dress as her mother walked through the house. Helen touched things to know how they felt and how they were shaped.

There must have been many things Helen wanted to do, many things she wanted to say, but she couldn't. Helen was often angry. She kicked, screamed, and cried.

Helen was also mischievous. Once she locked her mother in the pantry. Another time she cut off all her friend's hair.

Helen's parents took her to eye doctors. But nothing could be done to help Helen see again.

Then Helen's parents took her to Washington, D.C. to meet Alexander Graham Bell, the inventor of the telephone. Dr. Bell had once taught in a school for the deaf. He helped the Kellers find a teacher for Helen.

The teacher they found was Anne Mansfield Sullivan. Helen first met her on March 3, 1887. Helen called that day her "soul's birthday."

Helen was not an easy student. Once, in a fit of anger, she knocked out two of Anne Sullivan's teeth.

First Anne Sullivan taught Helen proper manners. Then she taught her words.

Anne used a finger alphabet. She gave Helen a doll and spelled "d-o-l-l" in the palm of Helen's hand. She gave Helen a hat and spelled "h-a-t" in her hand. But Helen did not understand.

One day Anne and Helen passed a water pump. Anne took Helen's hand and put it under the water. In Helen's other hand Anne spelled "w-a-t-e-r."

Now Helen understood. Everything has a name.

Helen wanted to learn more. That day she learned the words "mother" and "father." She also learned "teacher" which is what she called Anne Sullivan.

Many years later Helen Keller wrote that learning "water," her first word, gave her soul light, hope, and joy.

Helen learned hundreds, then thousands of words.

Soon Anne Sullivan taught Helen to read by feeling patterns of raised dots on paper. This kind of writing for the blind is called Braille.

Helen learned so much and so fast that she became famous throughout the world. She was called "the wonder girl."

When Helen was ten she decided she would learn to speak. But Helen couldn't hear the sounds she was making. She did learn to speak, but not clearly.

In 1900 Helen became a college student. She went to Radcliffe College. Anne Sullivan sat next to her and spelled in Helen's hand everything that was said in class. Helen was an excellent student. While she was in college, she wrote *The Story of My Life*, which was read by people throughout the world. Helen graduated with honors in 1904.

Helen wrote more articles and books about her life, her teacher, and how she learned. She and Anne Sullivan lectured before large audiences.

Anne Sullivan died on October 20, 1936. She had been with Helen for almost fifty years. After Anne's death, Polly Thomson, Helen's secretary since 1914, became her constant companion.

Helen worked all her life to help others, especially blind people. She worked for many years for the American Foundation for the Blind.

During the Second World War, Helen Keller visited injured soldiers in hospitals. Her visits meant a lot to the soldiers. Many of them had been blinded or had lost their hearing in the fighting. Helen Keller brought them hope. They would try to lead useful lives despite their disabilities, just like Helen Keller.

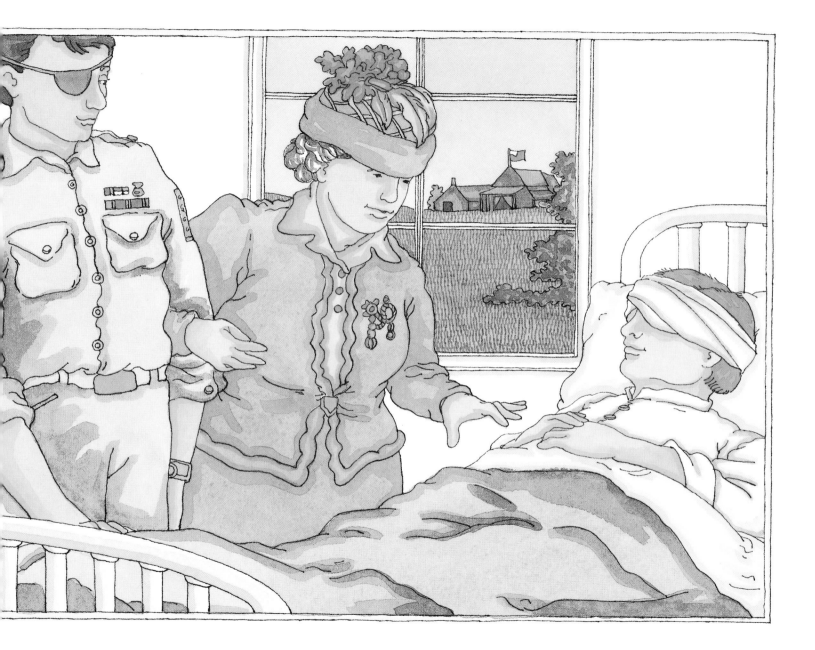

Important people wanted to meet Helen Keller. She met kings, queens, and presidents. She met actors, writers, and scientists.

People, universities and governments all over the world gave Helen Keller awards. In 1964 President Lyndon Johnson gave her the Presidential Medal of Freedom.

Helen Keller died on June 1, 1968.

Helen Keller couldn't see or hear, but for more than eighty years she had always been busy. She read and wrote books. She learned how to swim and even how to ride a bicycle. She did many things well. But most of all, Helen Keller brought hope and love to millions of disabled people.

IMPORTANT DATES

1880	Born on June 27 in Tuscumbia, Alabama.
1882	As a result of illness, became deaf and blind.
1887	Met Anne Sullivan.
1900	Entered Radcliffe College.
1924	Began to work for the American Foundation for the Blind.
1936	Anne Sullivan died on October 20.
1943–1946	Visited injured soldiers.
1964	Received the Presidential Medal of Freedom from President Lyndon Johnson.
1968	Died on June 1.